Volta

Flipping Life Over, Like It's

a Pancake

Part One

By Lil Fangs

Volta

Flipping Life Over, Like It's a Pancake

Part One

D.O.C.I.S. International

ISBN: 978-90-829-7-2

https://lilfangs.com

https://docis.international

CONTENTS

3

WHAT'S THE VOLTA?

By the time I've released the next part of this book, you and I will be living our best lives. That's the Volta.

The parallel between the term "volta" – a shift in a poem – and what we'll be doing here, is that the shift in life we'll initiate, will be mainly caused by writing. (Yes, something like that is possible!)

This book describes the steps that need to be taken, to flip life over, from, in my case, the dissatisfying, inconsistent rollercoaster it is now, to a joyful experience. My exact steps cannot be copied by anyone else, because they apply to my personal situation.

But the method I use to cause the shift, you can most certainly use to change around anything you want to tackle in your own life.

I don't believe in self-help books – unless what needs to be changed is that general and simple. I believe that no one can lead you to real insights and real change, but yourself. Only you know what satisfies you. The insights that lead to the awareness of what exactly needs to change and how, come from the inside.

Only you know and experience the way you feel. Sometimes perception can be so layered, that no words can explain someone's exact feelings. Translating that to a description for a friend, coach and/or therapist to understand, leaves room for many different forms of interpretation. A response is always influenced by their personal perception and personal experience.

In the end, you will put in the most effort in your change, and you walk that path alone. (Sure, with the support of those around you.) That's why only you can help yourself. And that is great!

It is great, because the satisfaction you'll get from your success, will last a lifetime, and no one can take that away from you, because it's your own creation.

Another great part, is that you're not alone, in this unique process of change. I am with you, every step of the way! And so will be the other people who can relate to this Volta.

The Method

It all starts with something "very old-fashioned": use pen and paper. Write down everything you think and feel, and please disregard every form of commentary you have ever heard.

This is something between you and yourself. It's important that you're completely honest and do not stick to any (unspoken) social rules you tend to conform yourself to.

If, for example, swearing is not accepted in your social environment, but you feel like swearing in your written honesty: you should swear. There are no limits here!

No one will comment on what you write down, because this is not intended for sharing. (You may share it, of course, but one might write differently – less pure – when it is to be shared with other people.)

The contents of your writing, might include things you can't easily talk about with other people, because not everyone might be able to relate to it, and they might not understand what you experience.

Please know that I can truly relate to how you feel, if you can relate to the previous sentence. Those hidden feelings require expression, and writing them down is enough! (There are many other things I can relate to as well.) I don't want you to feel lonely. If you do feel that way, by the end of reading this book, that will not even be possible (anymore)!

As you write this intense self-reflection down – maybe you already perceive this – you might experience a meditative state of introversion. (Many people say that disconnecting from the world is bad, but I disagree, and I'll explain why, in the chapter about social comfort.) Our high speed world doesn't stop, but your experience of self is timeless.

Your physical existence has grown a lot, since the moment you were born.

Mentally, you have matured a lot, throughout that process. But underneath all of that, in between your introspection and extrospection, the observant inner eye of yourself, has always stayed the same, is what I believe. It's that part of your being that makes you the unique individual you always have been.

By analyzing yourself in this way, without any guidance, you're taking yourself to a higher state of consciousness! You're doing this, without any guidance. All I can do is paint a general picture. Only you can tap into yourself.

Writing your perception down, is to create an overview of everything that is going on in your life: the state(s) of your emotions, what you experience in your daily occupations, how you (truly) feel about your daily occupations, your social circle, your love life, any media publications that (recently) got to you and influence your perception of life, the state of your finances and how that influences your emotions (if that's the case), any other internal experiences and/or external factors... With your writing, it's as if you make a picture of your life, frozen in time, while your actual perception isn't frozen in time.

You are completely free in the way you write down your reflection. You decide the layout and the way you begin and end it. This is the first step to creating your Volta.

When you have your "written picture" done – the length of it and time needed to write it, vary per person – the next step is to value it and reflect it to the long term.

All factors in your life, you've just captured on paper, should be reflected on again, individually. In this part of the process, for every single aspect of your life, you should ask yourself: "Does this contribute to my happiness?" "Is this healthy for me?" And reflect it to the long-term: "Do I want to keep this, as a part of me?"

That part of the reflection can be emotionally hard. You might confront yourself with things you've been (trying to) look away from. You might realize that you will have to change a lot about your life, in order to experience true happiness. (I'm not keeping a single aspect of my life the same!)

Never forget that it's for a very good cause. We're tackling all of it, for once and for all!

When you're done with all of the initial reflection – from writing your "written picture", to reflecting it to the long term – it is time to treat yourself, because you've just done something that requires a lot of mental strength and self-awareness.

Not everyone can reflect on his or her conscious like this. Especially in the way the initial reflection requires you to, so spoil yourself, directly after you're done! You deserve some extra relaxation! Buy yourself a gift, take some days off, soak yourself in a nice bath, get a massage, treat yourself to a nice dinner... Love yourself!! That's the most important part of being an individual.

Take a few days to let everything you've written down sink in. Especially because the next step, will be causing your own Volta... You will, perhaps with the assistance of the steps in the next chapters of this book, design a new life's path, which include your shift towards eternal happiness.

Many people believe that philosophical ideals, such as equanimity, or *apatheia*, are impossible to achieve. I believe that those states are achievable, when you're self-aware enough. As long as you assist yourself towards and maintain living circumstances, you can be fully at peace with, you can't go wrong on the path towards your ideal state of mind. That is what your path should lead you to: your ideal state of mind, which will last for all eternity. That is what this book might assist you in, in case you weren't there yet. It might not be easy, but it surely isn't impossible.

There are factors that can disturb us from the path we're on, we should curb. Primitive drives, for example.

Everyone has primitive drives. Those drives don't have to be something bad. They shouldn't be suppressed.

As long as you are above them, you can and should acknowledge and express them, in a rational manner, because they are a part of you and therefore shouldn't be pushed away, as long as they don't possess you. Through reason, this can be controlled.

Why I'm using present tense about myself, while I say that my method works?

Because my method has worked very well for me, in the past, but I have now extended it.

When I was going through a rough period, and I had no one who could relate to my feelings, I resorted to writing, and came out so strong that I was almost (literally) unrecognizable. I became the best version of myself.

Something I did not (have to) take into consideration, to solve that phase, were external factors. Writing and adapting myself to my findings, were enough for a Volta, back then.

My current one, includes redemption from false media publicity, naturally recovering from post-traumatic stress and tachycardia, freeing myself from (financial) dependency and harmful authorities, and creating a(n almost) completely new social circle.

That means that there are a lot of things need to happen, which require measures that go beyond writing with pen and paper, in theory. But maybe, just maybe, we could solve all of our problems, solely by writing strategically.

If I can get exactly enough people to read this book until the end, and follow the steps I describe, writing is all we need! If not: we will still succeed! It will only take a bit more time.

The coming chapters, describe the initial reasoning of my own Volta, followed by the description of my path. I explain all of my steps and ask you questions, by means of feeding your Volta, and touch on universal external factors. In the last chapter, we finalize our path. All of the discoveries this journey will bring, will fit together perfectly, and form a path.

If the components of my strategic writing fall in place perfectly, our paths to happiness will intertwine. That's what perfect happiness looks like, to me.

Even if it doesn't: I will be much closer to the right direction, and I will have grown a lot more. You will still

have designed your perfect path, and
will be able to walk it.

Let's have some fun, shall we?

SELECTING STATES

What do you want to feel, when you experience infinite happiness?

In this chapter, I'll break down the current state of my feelings and the factors that cause this, as well as the way in which I want them to change. The conclusion, I save, to later use it for the definition of my path.

My Volta is huge. A lot of factors in it, are external. It might come off as a total mess, but in the end, it's controlled. It will all become clear, as the Volta unfolds :-].

Today's "judgment culture" makes me suppress a lot of my emotions. Gossip, including the judgment of it, has become a serious business that is taken overly serious – referring to what is considered "important news" these days.

This culture is copied in small communities.

Big international broadcasts touch on, for example, that whoever has had sex with whoever – as if no one has ever had sex – and then they destroy that person's complete image with their judgment, because the public considers them a source of "unbiased information". And then it ends up in their topics of conversation.

On a smaller scale, the same thing happens. Neighbor A has had sex with neighbor C, and everyone discusses the rumors in full details. A conversation about a topic like that, is something I can never enjoy, because I consider it fucking irrelevant information. It might not even be true. But it's the standard in this life.

There are things to discuss, which are so much more important. I do not understand why unimportant "information" like that is appreciated by so many.

But of course, everyone has his or her own preferences. What I'm bothered by, is how lonely I am in my stance. I can't talk about this with anyone, because everyone follows this culture and defends it, like it's a religion.

I believe that there are people out there who think about all of this, the same way I do. But we're outnumbered and hard to find.

It seems like all regular people talk about, is anyone but themselves. I don't want people to discuss sensitive information about me, behind my back, and add all kinds of untruths to it. I am on a path of making serious global changes, and it's important that, in that process, people know who I truly am. Or at least that the people who I can be of service do, aren't encouraged to stay away from me, because of false rumors.

Before my false publicity, I already had a very strict "Never show any weakness" policy between me and myself, because it causes people to treat me with something that looks like respect. (Real respect is hard to get, when people are jealous of your intelligence.) I also don't like when very personal topics, are turned into jokes or casual topics of conversation, so I keep everything to myself. It made me the right person to share secrets with.

I would rather be seen as an advisory beacon, who has never experienced negative emotions, than be known as someone whose experience of life holds the juiciest gossip of self-

21

related drama. I was that beacon, surviving every social situation.

But that false bad publicity portrayed me as the emotionally weakest person on Earth – while that is far from the truth – and ever since that has been broadcasted, the only question I get is: "Are you feeling better now?" While I have never told anyone that I was feeling bad. I was not feeling the way that that statement which I didn't write, "told the masses how I felt".

I put so much effort into building up a proper reputation, for my career, and all of that disappeared at once. I'll summarize how these feelings, causing me to want a new Volta, emerged:

Not long after choosing my start-up business over university, and no one understanding my decision for quicker potential success, a fight with my parents about their disapproval of a client of mine, led to me silencing them and cropping up my anger, because the future of my company was at stake, and continuing the argument that went as far as all of us raising our voices, was pointless. They called me psychotic, because I had put my last faith for success in that client, and kept holding on to my belief, even when I wasn't allowed to leave the house anymore, and it was clear that their interference and limitations – considered "good parenting" – were going have severe consequences for my life and my business.

Not much later, I was trying to free myself from the unwanted psychiatric surveillance my relatives got me stuck into, while trying to have no one finding out about it.

No matter how often I told those psychiatrists that it's none of their business what I think of and believe, because all they want to do is search for a good ground to call me crazy, and mentioning they were contributing to the pain I felt, with their indirect insults about how they believe that I need help... No matter how often I begged them to leave me alone, and that I'll live a regular 9 – 5 or go back to school when they're not monitoring me anymore, because them in my life would create a false image of who I am...

They kept visiting me and forcing me to talk, threatening to give me a warrant, if I kept refusing their therapy and their pills. And instead of helping me, my parents forced me to do the same thing. All I felt was anger, but expressing that would get me a warrant for sure.

The day that I gave in to taking those antipsychotics, so that I could go outside, was the day I never wanted to go home again. (Giving someone antipsychotics, while you're not even sure about what's going on with that person, should be illegal.) There was no other way I could get those psychiatrists off my back.

The hell that followed, where I was reported missing, while I was alone outside for three days contemplating suicide, missing my client, was interrogated by police over and over and over and over and over again, while in the meantime a false statement about me went viral and people whom I thought I could trust portrayed me as a mentally weak person, sealed my downfall.

I told those cops that whatever they do, they should not send me home to my parents, and that they should help me reach my client, because I would rather go to prison, than go home. But they, too, did not listen to me, and sent me home to my parents, after which the psychiatric hell continued in an even worse manner.

By means of getting a second opinion – because I want my records to show the truth about me, for my politics related business aspirations – I later let myself be taken into a mental institution, on a voluntary basis, to prove that I shouldn't be under surveillance.

There, like anywhere else, they said that they really want to do what's good for me et cetera. I fell for it, that time, because it was my final hope of getting out of that surveillance. All they wanted to do, was finish what their colleagues started. Their colleagues couldn't label me with a mental illness, after interrogating me for more than 6 months, because the only reason I was having those therapy sessions, was that my parents wanted me to talk after I silenced them, and they then "wanted to know what happened". (What happened, is that I found it pointless to continue to talk to them.)

They couldn't DSM label me, because there was nothing to label. (Yet still they had the nerve to tell me that I need their awful conversation and pills "to get better".) But after the institution, the "findings" in my records went to "her parents think she's psychotic", to "she's a schizophrenic with a learning disability". Their grounds for that conclusion were the following: I told them that I quit my studies, to focus on my business, after three months "already", I believe that I can positively change our global system and I still kept talking about that client, who was more than just a client, because experience that I share something supernatural with him.

I do not agree with those diagnoses at all. I was there to prove my sanity. (Or to prove that they have caused my post-traumatic stress, but no psychiatrist would write him or herself down as the cause of someone's "mental illness".)

That learning disability is complete fucking nonsense, because I have graduated from the highest level of high school in the Netherlands [my first language is Dutch… I graduated from het gymnasium], my IQ was measured 133 when I was 6, I obtained certificates from The Open University, in Mathematics and Statistics, while I never attended a class and travelled and worked during the curriculum, and dropping out of Erasmus University was a decision, because I needed a faster way to comfortably move out of my parents' house fast, because their nonsense was driving me crazy (way before the psychiatry already), so I chose to bet on my start-up, and the list goes on...

That being confident about having the intelligence to make a change, is considered a symptom, is just... That more than half of the population on this planet, believes that the world is a dystopia, and that it will stay that way, doesn't make it a fact? I find that psychotic?

If some drug addict who isn't capable of doing anything, states that he's Jesus or Elijah, and they want to give that person that diagnosis, then enfin, I wouldn't have much to bring up against that.

But I have a strategy! I have a serious strategy! I haven't explained it to them, because they haven't asked – and they wouldn't even be able to understand it – but I have a serious strategy! The pessimistic view of the psychiatrist(s) shouldn't be a ground for that diagnosis. It has ruined my records.

All I need to put it into practice, are some people with serious brains, who can follow the theoretical side of my lead, and some good investors. I'll elaborate on this throughout the rest of the book, because of course, this is the Volta!

And my thoughts and feelings about my client, I kept to myself for so long, because I knew that it was controversial. I never intended to share it with anyone, but now that it has led to that diagnosis...

"My client" is my former professor in microeconomics: Dr. Crutzen. The first time I saw him, I noticed that my reasoning and his actions, seemed extraordinarily in sync – as if he can hear my thoughts, and that I'm very attracted to him, despite our age difference. I felt comfortable being myself around him, and was very happy when he responded positively to my request about making a campaign for him.

The day the fight with my parents started, which ended up with me silencing them, was the first day that my skull started to move, without me controlling that movement. With every move, I hear his voice saying something. I told those psychiatrists, when I was finally honest about this, after more than 6 months, that I enjoy being able to talk to him through reason.

My honesty was solely because I was getting tired of their surveillance. I initially kept to myself, because my belief sounds like something for a psychiatric diagnosis.

I explained to them that I do not want his voice out of my head and that I tell them this, in that "research hospital", because, according to the scientific method, they can't prove that I experience a false reality, without hearing that from Dr. Crutzen himself. Only when he says: "No, I cannot hear her thoughts," and/or "No, I am not able to perform brain-to-brain communication," their ground to diagnose me with schizophrenia is scientifically correct. If not, all of my sense perceptions are true.

I asked them to allow me to invite him over, or that they invite him over themselves, to conduct an experiment I had written out, to confirm or falsify my case. Concepts such as reading minds and brain-to-brain communication, aren't scientifically proven, but that doesn't mean that they're impossible. I'm sure that most people don't have the capacity to experience something like that, but that doesn't mean that there are exceptions, with a different anatomy.

They were not open to that, and wanted me to try a new brand of antipsychotics. I told them that I did not want to do that, and I appealed to my right to leave the institution, because I was in that closed vicinity of that institution, to prove my case, and they did not want to cooperate.

They found that I did not want to cooperate, and they didn't allow me to leave. I was trapped there. Only by taking those new antipsychotics – they experimented with three types – and "showing progress" in the process "of suddenly not experiencing the movement of my skull anymore", I was allowed to leave.

All of the people I used to hang out with, who came to visit me, after I hadn't seen them in months (almost a year, for many), asked me: "Oh my god, what happened?" after having missed out on a year of traumatic experiences. On a very high pace – it becomes a routine, after having seen more than ten people in a week, who ask me to summarize all of my experiences, for as long as their span of attention lasts – I touched on everything that happened, but left the brain-to-brain communication aspect out of the story, and concluded it with that I am held there against my will, while I shouldn't be, and that I needed a "non-schizophrenic" to defend my case, so that I could leave. They all said things like: "Well, that's too bad. But it's just a medical file. Just let it happen, and let it go." "Just take that medication, it's for a good cause. I know it sucks, but you'll get better." "We were all so worried about you! You're making everyone worried by going missing and having strange things going on in your mind. *Continues to explain "worry" in full detail*" (If you're truly worried, where the fuck were you all year? Why am I summarizing twelve months in ten minutes? What the fuck kind of viral message did you share? If I would have considered your help useful, back then, I would have asked for it, but I didn't. Get the message?)

I attempted suicide in that same institution, because it seemed like I was going to spend the rest of my life under psychiatric surveillance. Every therapy session started with: "Do you still hear the voice of Benoît Crutzen in your head?" Of course, they want to hear me say, "No," after taking a few of those antipsychotics. That lie could have gotten me to freedom, but I stayed honest, because otherwise, they would believe that their quackery works on me. They also considered me breaking contact with my parents, after being transferred from a regular hospital, to a mental institution, a reason to keep me there.

Not long after my suicide attempt, and getting back in touch with my parents, I was allowed to go to the open vicinity. (It basically works the same as the prison system.) There, I was allowed to leave, after promising to continue to live under the surveillance of the "home psychiatrists" who had been monitoring me months before. Of course, my parents insisted the same thing, AGAIN.

"Sure," I told them. But a few months after that, when their surveillance started to drive me so crazy, I managed to book a one-way flight to the United States, without anyone knowing. [Not long before that, I started my blog: LilFangs.com.]

I intended to start a new life there, but ran out of money. My mother bought me a ticket to come back to the Netherlands, when I was about to not be able to afford a roof above my head anymore. (That I crossed the border without anyone noticing, but managed to do damage control – so not another viral nonsense campaign – by posting a letter to my parents' house on the day I left, in which I wrote that I left and why I left, which arrived the next day, physically distanced me from them well enough, but doesn't take away that texting exists.)

Paying for meals was already not possible anymore, in that period. On my worst day, all I ate were 10 spicy popcorn nuggets from Burger King, for which I paid about $1.98.

After coming back, I started working full-time, I had my final exams, I started this publishing company, and many more other time consuming occupations, which didn't leave any room for psychiatric surveillance. That's why I chose to occupy myself with all of those things, while I, truthfully, was so exhausted from my trip to The States.

Not long after that, I sought medical assistance in Germany, found out that those antipsychotics have been damaging my heart, and that there still are a lot of physical symptoms that need to be tackled, had a lot of conflicts at home, have been kicked out plenty of times in a row, lived in Berlin for a very short while, in a relationship that was one of the worst social experiences of my life, and now, today, as I'm writing this, I'm staying with family friends, because getting kicked out every time makes me too uncertain about having a roof above my head, without having a dime to spend, and I want certainty about having a bed to sleep in. (More details about what I had to endure, can be read in *The Unpublished Episodes of*

Nosce Te Ipsum I, followed by the article *180 Days of Fangs*, on <u>LilFangs.com</u>.)

This experience has permanently damaged me. I used to be overly positive about mankind. I used to feel love for everyone I came across. I used to say that my purpose in life is to make life even better, for every single being on Earth.

But ever since that abuse of authority I've been subjected to, followed by that negative publicity, by which everyone I used to trust, sealed my abandonment and left me for dead, my view on life has changed. Irreversibly.

Some people don't think further than that gossip business and the routines of life, and their vision will never be broadened, because they don't even want that. Including them in my attempt to improve the quality of life, is a waste of time, because they're not even aware of their own consciousness. (What's the point of putting in so much effort, while they don't even do that for themselves, while it's not my responsibility and while they'll probably just criticize it and take it for granted?)

When my change of view on life was recent, I felt the chest pains of (self-)grief, continuously, because I was shocked and disappointed. I was also very worried about my future, because I had a start-up in PR, which didn't survive the after-effects of that false publicity, and that was all I had.

The way that abuse of authority – from relatives, the police and the (Dutch) psychiatric system – and media nonsense have taken away my trust in people, causes me to feel stress, every time I talk to someone. I keep thinking: *"You don't see the real me. You believe*

41

that I'm that person from that nonsensical message you shared. (If you truly knew me, you wouldn't have shared it.)" This stress contributes to the tachycardia I have.

Communication has become a chess game for me, because I fear being subjected to that same situation again. It has been tried again, subjecting me to that awful authority. Plenty of times. By publishing this book, either they or I, depending on its interpretation and success, will be checkmated.

The way I currently express myself in the physical realm, comes from my brain and not from my heart. I'm too busy reasoning out: *"Responding this, insinuates this, and will thus lead to this reaction. I don't want to end up being hurt by pessimism, because no one believes in real prosperity and real talents these days, and people have*

been trying to debunk my statements
about better days so very often already,
so what response hides that belief of
mine, will be my response." That has to
change. I want to express my true self,
but I want to feel safe, when I do. The
feeling of safety is caused by trust, and
for that trust, I need a completely new
social circle, which consists of like-
minded people.

Currently, the after-effects of the
traumatic experience of my (recent)
past, cause a constant fear for the same
trauma. I'm afraid my parents'
disapproval of my behavior, will
incentivize them to start that psychiatry
shit again. They have mentioned it
quite often already, in the past few
months.

The abuse of authority, has
awakened a lot of hidden anger, from
the way I've been treated against my

will, without being able to say anything back. That anger becomes worse, when people say [especially my father] that that psychiatric hell, was what I deserved. It also becomes worse from seeing or hearing reminders from that traumatic experience I've been living through, and hearing people talk about superficial things as if they're serious. But that anger only results itself in tachycardia. I haven't attacked anyone, and I don't intend to, because even though it might feel satisfying, that feeling is only there as a result of my trauma, and using violence without a safety net, will make that worse. (Indirectly saying that I would feel no remorse, but I'm trying to only give you good, exemplary ideas here!)

Before I summarized my trauma, I mentioned that I don't like it when personal issues become a casual topic of conversation. Unfortunately, since that bad publicity, that is all people "know about me", and that is all I can talk about with people in my current social circle, because they don't like my work, and I don't care about gossip and TV shows. It's frustrating that my entire process is internal, and they don't even know about most of it, but our philosophies on life differ so much, staying unaffected by their input, will lead to a much greater merit.

A lot of people treat me like I'm crazy, because all they see is that I've gone from an extrovert to an introvert. My next step is to enhance my introversion even further, because all I care about, is my path in life, and those who only bother me with their harsh critique and diminishing advice, are a negative influence.

Now, when I talk, move or do anything else, I still tell myself to act the way regular people act, and hide the fact that, to this day, my skull still moves in synch with every syllable Dr. Crutzen transfers to me.

To avoid commentary, in the physical realm, I suppress every aspect of my personality that makes me unique. I don't even sing when I feel like doing that, because going flat or starting with the wrong couplet, can result into other people laughing, and my voice is a very sensitive part of my self-expression.

My Volta can only begin to shape itself, when I have tapped into myself far enough that only I can influence my emotions, and whatever humans in my extroversion do, it won't get to me.

I've been there. Physically and emotionally. And every time someone tried to hurt me, I listed so many arguments about why they're wrong, they often weren't even able to go into it. But after those false rumors, the counter argument has become: "Yeah, but you're a schizophrenic and I'm not," and all I can return to that is silence, because they have no fucking clue what they're talking about, and raising my voice and attacking that person without ever being able to stop, is punishable.

When I regard to the feelings I have for these external parties – I used to care about them a lot – as something that should not be a part of me anymore, and only listen to myself, only then, I can initiate the emotional shift that will make me feel eternal happiness.

The feelings I've listed in these past few paragraphs, including their cause, are: sadness, grief, fear, loneliness, stress, distrust, anger and the strategic conscious suppression of my true personality, in the physical realm. After my Volta, I, of course, don't want to feel any of this again.

First, I'll state what could make these feelings disappear permanently, and then I'll list the feelings I do want to feel.

In my personal case, most solutions solve more than one negative feeling at once. Usually, solutions don't have to be that drastic, but my solution can only be drastic, and I'll tell you why.

Distance will solve most of my problems. Taking distance from the people who can have such a negative impact on the way I feel. This goes against everything today's social culture stands for, and even goes against Biblical commandments –

because this includes plenty of relatives – but in the end, what matters the most, is that I don't have to suffer anymore.

When I don't have to look those who consider me a schizophrenic, in the eyes again, a lot of anger, sadness, distrust, fear and grief, will never surface again. I will never have to endure superficial conversations again, with people who think that their minds are somehow superior to mine. I have nothing in common with those people [not even music!!!], so it's a miracle that we have been that close in the first place.

It's drastic to leave a whole life in a community behind, but it excites me so much. It will also allow me to focus on my path much better. I'll elaborate on that, in the next chapter.

If taking distance is a solution to you, too, then the same goes for you! You should never suffer! God does not want you to suffer! (Who came up with the opposite, is awful...) Let's become best friends :D. More about that in the coming chapters.

The next feelings to tackle, are my feeling of loneliness, and the need I feel to suppress my true personality, as well as making sure that all bad feelings don't return.

I hope that my method to intertwine paths, which is what the climax of this book leads to, will solve this. I need to find like-minded people, whose paths are similar to mine, since my path is what is on my mind the most. It's what's most excitable to me.

The similarity in our personalities, should be that we don't have a sense of humor that includes laughing about other people's misery, because I find that immoral, and my new friend should feel the same about that. The people I'll bond with and keep in my life for all eternity, should be people who will truly never harm me, the way I'll truly never harm them. We should stand up for each other, when we need to. We should support each other, and empower each other.

When I'm surrounded by people who are like that, like me, I'll feel safe – more than emotionally – and the boundary, related to my self-expression in real life, will disappear.

Finding these people is, unfortunately, not guaranteed. But I will never stop searching! Fighting for myself, in this way, contributes to feeling better as well.

The feelings I want to have are inner harmony, continuous arousal and radiance. It was what I experienced when I was at my best, after my previous Volta. My coming Volta, will make me feel like that, but then even better:

Inner harmony

Whatever comes on my path, by reason, it will never cause stress. I have now endured enough to know how to anticipate anything from distracting me from the path that I'm on. In an extreme case, I know that I'll have people I can count on.

My heart rate will not be on level tachycardia anymore. No social situation will re-initiate this. No individual will get on my nerves.

The peaceful state I'll be in, will make it possible for me to really enjoy the perception of life.

Continuous arousal

It doesn't take much, for me to start to feel love for someone. It doesn't take much for me to fall in love.

If I succeed on my path, everything about life will be attractive to me. I'll look around, when I'm outside, and feel so overwhelmed by all of the beauty I see, in people and in architecture. Everything about life will turn me on.

I've been there. Before I endured that grief I felt after I realized that life isn't what I thought it was, I used to be so wet all of the time, that I was able to masturbate without using my hands. I call it laking (as in lake-ing, from the wetness).

I could look (attractive) people in the eyes and feel penetration. The playfulness in our conversation, would increase this feeling, so much that – (unfortunately¿) I suppressed this in my movement and verbal expression –

it would have been hearable in my voice, if I wouldn't have given it a limit.

Seeing the passion and ambition in people, and other unique things in nature, always made me feel so happy. Now that I've grown a little older and have become a lot wiser, I can't see life in that same way anymore.

I've realized that most people's words, related to passion and ambition, are just a script for a higher salary, and have nothing to do with real passion, which is priceless. And after re-realizing the relationship between global warming propaganda, and the way the Netherlands are constructed below sea level, all I see when I'm outside, is an overpopulated, unnatural, dilapidated chaos, which should have never ended up as the mess that it is.

Life doesn't attract me anymore, the way it used to attract me. But meeting people who think about this the same way as I do, might re-initiate that spark, and give me back my laking, which I miss so much...

I'm not the type of person for a monogamous relationship – I learnt after my first and last monogamous relationship. I fall in love too fast for that.

If you're truly ambitious, for the goal you have in life, and it relates to societal reform, to me, you have it all. We'll have a very strong connection.

My love goes deep and is eternal. It can never be limited to just one person.

I don't want to think about my attraction to someone else, when I'm in a monogamous relationship, because it's disruptive to me, and hurtful to the other.

(The concept of having an individual as your sole emotional possession, sounds a bit unnatural to me, after having experienced it. The attachment and isolation can't be part of the purpose of life, I think. Sure, heterosexual people can make children, naturally. But that can't be what life is meant for. To keep up that routine of providing for the people within your isolation. It also causes overpopulation and overconsumption... Even the normal banana is extinct, in this country... (Which is, from a natural perspective, just cold sea, so it shouldn't even have banana's in the first place.) That shouldn't be found normal.)

I want to be able to express the love I feel for everyone I feel love for. And to be able to receive love from them (if it's there). Without thinking: "Don't do it. My boyfriend won't appreciate that. His wife won't appreciate that."

If your personality is similar to mine, and we meet, me falling in love with you is inevitable... Regardless of your gender, race or age: it's going to happen. I've been without someone I can truly relate to, for so long... I can't stand being so alone. I don't want to feel like this anymore.

What would be the most ideal, to me, is becoming polygamous. I want everyone I feel eternal love for, to be in my life for all eternity. (That is illegal in the Netherlands, but I don't intend to grow old here. That's not even possible, with the high speed the water level rises with.)

I never want to live that fixed routine of having to provide for a family that consists of parents and children. Where I have to live a fixed routine, because my children go to school wherever – I found the first years of primary school the most awful, and would truthfully never want to send my child to such a place, with such barbarian children and teachers. Everything you have taught your child, might vanish at once, because of the teacher's authority and your child being subjected to group behavior.

We should just focus on eternal love, and fixing this system that will collapse, if we don't step in... Mutual attraction, without the drama that comes with the idea of possession, makes that process a lot more fun :-].

Radiance

Truthfully, there's no word for this type of energy, I want to feel again. It's that type of excitement that literally makes you want to smile and dance around, at some moments.

I've chosen radiance to name this feeling, because it feels like there are coming sun rays out of my body, which energizes the people around me as well. It's that type of energy that makes an entire audience feel excited, when you're on stage.

It shows itself as a motivating type of confidence, and gives you a little bit of power. Because every word you say, with that radiance, leads to a positive response.

I'll get this feeling again, when I'm further down my path, once I find that I can call myself successful (again).

Zoom in to your feelings:

What kind of feelings do you have often?

Do you enjoy these feelings?

What is the best way to make the feelings you don't enjoy, vanish?

Are there feelings you currently don't have, which you do want to have?

What should change, for you to be able to perceive those wanted feelings?

By answering these questions, you answer the lead question of this chapter.

SOCIAL COMFORT

What does your ideal social life look like?

As you might have noticed, I'm not very enthusiastic about the social norm in our society. I'll end this chapter with my solution to that, and will start with the description of my ideal social life.

In a social life that is ideal to me, my love life, my professional life and my friendships, are united as one. I'll be in love with my best friends, who are my partners in business.

Together, we rule over our empire. This is all drama-free, because I can't fucking stand drama over nothing.

We are all passionate about each other and our business is our child, so everything we do, is to ensure our survival.

The number of individuals in my social circle, should be enough to run an empire, intimately.

Only those who can hear me reason, should be an influential part of this. Only them, I trust enough, to give my heart to. I'm confident that we will build an amazing empire.

Only they are able to truly understand me, and the unique strategy I have in mind, for the expansion of my business. (You know that that's what I'm trying do here...)

We never stay in the same place for too long, because we like diversity. Our profession encourages this. (And so will nature, at some point.) But we have one place, we consider our home...

There will be a great variety in the types of project in our career. In this way, we'll never get bored with our occupation, and we'll challenge all of our unique talents.

My ideal social life, includes new traditions. After 22 years of celebrating Christmas, I've had enough of it. I don't want to do that until past my retirement.

I don't want to be confronted with deep-rooted traditions like that anymore. They're only there, because they're blended into our economic cycle. The sentimental motive behind it, is just marketing. I'm not feeling it...

The alternative I would like to propose, includes new festivities every year. More about that in the next chapter.

I need a completely new social circle, to live the social life I want to live. Everyone in my current social circle – or maybe I should say past social circle, because ever since that trauma, I've been spending most of my days all alone – strictly conforms him or herself to society's social norm.

Distancing myself from that, will go without any dramatic exchange of words. I'll just disappear again, the same way I've done that six times after that false publicity. No one knew. No one truly cares. Those sentimental words are just a formality.

It's no use talking about it. The doctrine that defines society's social norm, includes belief in certain ideas, which are considered facts, but I'll just never be able to adapt my stance to that.

You'll never genuinely hear the following nonsensical beliefs of society out of my mouth:

"We'll all human, we all make mistakes."

"Truly knowing yourself is never possible."

"There will never be peace."

"I wanted to become an astronaut. Now, I'm a bus driver. I'm living a happy life."

"Everyone can teach you something."

"Socializing in a public place is one of the most fun things in life."

"As long as I don't have to put in much effort."

"I just want to have a lot of money, so that I won't have to work and will be able to buy whatever I want."

"Powerful people want to make our experience of life like hell." (I used to say this, but that was more because I let other people's argumentation get to me. I do still consider myself a pawn. But someone spending a lifetime ruling over a society, just to hear people complaining about him/her, doesn't make sense to me anymore. The same goes for teachers...)

"Always settle for the least, because that makes you a good person."

"We'll never fully understand the universe."

I do not understand how people can firmly believe and defend that we are "randomly" born into a dystopia, and that life will stay this dystopia forever.

I agree that we're living in a dystopia. Nevertheless, it can't stay like this for all eternity. It's too destructive to nature.

But of course, if you don't mind spending your entire life span in front of the television, having superficial conversations and getting intoxicated when it all becomes too much, then I can understand why people settle for that simplistic belief.

The beliefs I listed 4 paragraphs ago, are considered science. There are dozens of people who blurt out that life will stay this awful routine, because some scientists have scientifically proven this. What the fuck? Did they get paid for that? Where can I find those publications?

Sure, you don't even need to do research, to see that most people are not intelligent enough to change the world. The constructions in our life are so fixed, it's a great challenge to change them. (By constructions, I do not only mean literal the constructions, which are harmful to nature, with their existence and emission. (Before you know it, all of the Earth will be built full? And then? (For this generation, not literally, but let's think ahead. If mankind continues on this pace...)) I also mean the system we were born into. The mechanism that combines concepts of economics, law, politics, et cetera. I'll get back to this, in the next chapter.)

Most of the people on Earth, are not capable of making the changes we need, for this planet to not cease to exist. Most of them, don't even try to think of solutions. They just say that there is no solution. The bar in our society is set extremely low, and, with the continuous existence and power of social media, it becomes even lower every day.

I state this as a series of facts, because if this weren't true, that essential change, would have been made already. Global warming and threats of bombings wouldn't have been a thing anymore.

Nature's clock is ticking. The sea level rises faster than "science" expects it to. This will get worse, because every day, laws are bent to allow businesses to exploit nature's goods. And when those goods have gone extinct, an artificial alternative is offered. That cannot be the purpose of nature. People have no clue what they're messing with. Can we hit the pause button on capitalism?

Especially in the Netherlands – but I'm writing this in English, mainly because of the success of SBS6, so any type of assistance will be highly appreciated – we need to start thinking of a plan for when the bathtub-like (non-)ecological construction of the country, succumbs to the water... If society continues their routine on this pace – why would they ever stop – that might happen faster than you think.

If there were someone out there, who could prevent this, and who would know a solution to the routines we have to conform ourselves to and the violence we come across, I assume that person would have done something by now.

I kept myself from any news and other trends, when I was under severe psychiatric surveillance. All I focused on was trying to not lose it, strategizing my way out of it, and coming up with a way to save my business (strategy for the long term).

After being released from the institution, I tried to "act more human", by meeting up with old friends and keeping up with news and trends again, so that I could engage in conversations, and make sure that no one had a ground to get me under more severe surveillance again. I was shocked by what I experienced.

After a year, only one thing had changed. Everything else was still the same.

Still, there are the overly dramatic headlines about President Trump, the idealizing of Bitcoins, and so on... "Funny videos" of less than a minute, are also still a big hype (and a big business)...

I expected to see new things. What a disappointment. People still treat the re-creations of the same concept, as if they're new. "New news." "A new smartphone." "A new movie." But what aspects of them are truly new?

I even feared that I would have competitors. That there would be any other young, self-educated, multi-talented person with a unique business strategy, which includes a strategy for societal reform.

Sure, there are a lot of "new" businesses from young people and there are plenty of newly discovered artists, but what they do is all very different from what I do.

On the one hand, that was quite a relief. The path to my monopoly is still (quite) clear. On the other hand, it makes me feel lonely, that things are propagated as new, and that I see everyone treat it as such, while, in my eyes, it really isn't. I can't act excited about such things (anymore). (When they were new to me, I was able to.)

Nothing has changed, except for one thing: the social norm has become harsher than ever. In the publications of any type of medium, before my isolation, there was still a tiny bit of love, visible in them. Now it's all heartless critique. It has even become humor.

A news source should be unbiased, because it has an (accessible more easily than school) educative role in society. When it's prejudiced, the masses take over their opinion, and consider it a fact. And that's what's happening. That's one of the reasons why there are so many people world-wide, reciting "anti-Trump" propaganda.

Out of nowhere, someone can extensively tell you or someone else, why something about anyone's appearance is not right. As if it matters.

Or why someone's performance is bad. As if it's not fully subjective and unasked for. My father, for example, out of nowhere, told me that I shouldn't find it strange that I'm broke, "Because LilFangs.com is terrible."

Sure, that heartlessness has always been a thing, especially since the TV show "Idols". But now, boosted on the internet, and visible in real life, it has escalated so far. We're now rating people by swiping and "always giving people helpful feedback" (while it's actually useless harsh critique).

Even though being socially active and "networking" are encouraged, I stay by myself, as much as possible. (In the past, it was different. I socialized as much as possible, until, after so much searching, I realized that there's no one like me, here.)

It's very important to be the best companion of yourself. Not only to stay in control over good feelings, because you are then the only influence: you never know when you have to survive under extreme circumstances. You (will) have to love yourself to survive something like that.

Your ambitions and path in life are unique. This is something you experience by yourself. Only you see the world through your eyes. Only you experience the feelings in your body. It should be joyful. It's your life.

"Get out there and make some friends," is the advice of many parents and what some modern propaganda (indirectly) insinuates. What I've learnt, from experience, is that friendships based on causality and friendships made for the sake of making friends, are not an addition to my path. They might (have) be(en) fun, but they're not fruitful. I still feel alone most of the time, and I still have no one I can explain my strategies to.

To me, a fruitful friendship is one where you share the same ambitions. I believe in guild-like friendships. Part of my method is to speed up the process of getting these.

My ambition is to set out a strategy that will change and improve – my definition of improvement, isn't based on the abundance of resources (anymore), but on the long-term sustainability of nature – the world.

This is considered psychotic, by the masses. It is considered impossible, by "science", they say.

How about we turn the eagerness for real change into science? Then, we cause a shift in paradigm. Believing in the Volta of Earth's dystopia, can then not be considered psychotic anymore.

If I can find more than 1,000 people in this country, who want to see and put effort into real large-scale global change, then it's a local scientific fact.

When I can find more than 10,000 people in more than one country, who believe the same thing, it's a global scientific fact.

Sure, for a better display of the population, the individuals of my sample shouldn't be hand-picked. But this time, I'll be speaking for an outnumbered group of people.

We should have the freedom to be ourselves, without being ridiculed by people who are barely conscious. It shouldn't affect us, but it does. That's because we know how to love. We want to feel mutual love, but this world is a very loveless place.

Unification is what we need. Let's separate ourselves from these mindless barbarians, and build a better world of our own. I already have the blueprints! Now is that psychotic, or is that new science? Are you with me? :D

It doesn't feel right to exclude people – who might not have read this book or might not be able to understand it. But they would destroy the new world, too, anyway.

The new routine of life will require much more effort and reasoning, because environmentally harmful concepts, such as the supermarket, will cease to exist, as well as prepackaged foods.

They will never accept that, even though it's way healthier. And I don't want fraud in my alternative system, so...

The new system I have in mind, is parallel to the current system, and the people in it, are hand-picked, by recruitment.

I really hope I can make you excited for the plans for the societal Volta I have in mind!

As for the general idea behind this chapter: get comfortable and close your eyes. Imagine the version of you, in a state of eternal happiness, with the feelings you've listed in the previous chapter. That awesome individual in action: how do you interact with others?

How do they interact with you?

What do you do together?

What's the difference between the social life you've imagined, and your current social life?

What would take that difference away?

That's how you answer the lead question of this chapter.

POWER

How much power do you really want in life?

The system we were born into, is what leads us, currently. That's how I see it.

I was born and raised in Rotterdam, in the Netherlands, so I have the Dutch nationality, I've been subjected to the Dutch education system, over everything I pay tax to the Dutch government, and in my actions, I'm obliged to conform myself to the Dutch law. It doesn't matter if I want all these things or not: I don't have a choice.

If I'd say: "But I don't want to be part of the financial system at all," or "But I don't want to have a nationality at all," I wouldn't be able to survive, in the way our system is constructed. Globally. I would not be able to get access to resources, and I would not be able to travel.

To get access to resources, I need money, and to get money, I need to work. I had to go to school, to get a qualification for a (good) job, I need to earn with, so that I can pay for my basic needs, and spend money on what I consider enjoyable. Everyone in the world is subjected to this "chain of decision making", which ends as a routine to earn money. It's how we're forced to spend our time.

Meanwhile, there are tons of businesses that provide us with all kinds of services and resources, and the government is there to guide that process as a whole. (We could have an endless discussion about what the role of the government is, and if it's necessary to have a government in the first place. It's all very controversial.

(And I think the power of the government should be limited to only technocratic influence, related to the long-term sustainability of Earth, but that the specialists, who usually are the advisors, should be the ones in charge.))

We're all born into this enormous global mechanism. The system itself, encourages us to choose a spot in it – as, for example, a doctor, who cures sick people and makes it possible for them to get back in the race, or as a bus driver, who helps getting people from A to B, when they are, for example, about to go somewhere to earn money, or to do something for recreation – by the propaganda in its education system and media.

When the system started to take shape, ages ago, the catastrophic consequences of the disruption of

Earth's ecosystem and the extinction of its resources, were not taken into consideration. Not in a sustainable way, to say the least.

Now, this path to destruction is sealed, by the global competition among businesses and governments. Instead of working together, there is a battle over market shares and being the richest.

Costs are considered more important than quality, profits are considered more important than sustainability. Everything "has to" become more, bigger and cheaper.

The effects of competition can have you on top of the list, the one day, and out on the street on the other. We are born into this race. Some as pawns, some as players.

In my view, especially since the internet, the meaning of the value of

money, has become far more abstract.
Digital things have value.

Crypto currencies escalate this. You
can own a total of $2,000 the one day,
and $2,000,000 on the other, just by
investing in the right one, so to speak.
The amount of work you have done for
this profit – disregarding the part of
saving up, because that does not have
to be with a specific purpose in mind –
is as much as clicking a few buttons
and filling out some fields. And with
that profit, you get access to so much of
Earth's resources, without having to do
anything in return.

In that way, with the many more
profit related loopholes in the system,
like that one, we speed up the process
of causing's the Earth's destruction.

Ignorance is the greatest catalyst.
There are still plenty of people who
contribute to this process, without even

being aware of it. They are the pawns of the entertainment industry, where its heavy competition, is now controlled by having the most valued gossip.

Some of people believe that that five meter wave, flooding the Netherlands, is not a concern for this generation. (But even when it isn't, why not still try our best to rid ourselves from the general existence of that threat?)

Creating a new system, will be inevitable, at some point, because our current regime of overconsumption and overpopulation, causes our current system to destroy itself at some point, and no one might even know, because everyone is too infatuated by the mechanism we live in now.

The system should change, rapidly. I want to grow old and grey without any trouble of nature. (Or of financial markets. Especially because I'm not personally involved in stock trading, but it's clear the new internet bubble(s) will burst at some point.) And I don't want to be a pawn, led by the power of someone else, again, when there is a truly sustainable solution put into practice. I want to direct the construction the new system myself. I want to know the system in and out. I don't want to be the victim of generations of other people's (conscious, self-preservative) mistakes, again.

I want to be the Praesens of the parallel system I have in mind, tasked with the overall guidance of the creation process, as well as being the correspondent of the leadership that will rule over it.

But currently, all "power" I have, is the right to vote, which is, of course, absolutely nothing. Chiefly, because of the power I want to have.

I have the knowledge to cause the shift that is needed, but I don't have the money to initiate it. I'm a pawn. An income and the right network, since I'm in need of specialists, for that new leadership, will change that.

It will also change how powerless I currently am, when it comes to having a roof above my head. I have access to my room, until my father finds that I'm not following his rules, and then I'm out on the street, which costs me savings. I don't have the money to say: "My house, my rules." Not yet...

To answer the lead question of this chapter, please answer the following questions:

Are you satisfied with the way you have control over the way you spend your time?

In our current system, which is finite, are you satisfied with the amount of influence you have in the way it is governed? Or should that be more, or less? If it should become more or less, how should it become more or less?

Do you prefer to have a leader, or be a leader?

If our current system would change, which eventually is inevitable, what do you want to influence in that process?

THE RIGHT OCCUPATION

What's your life's purpose?

The debate about the lead question of this chapter, is enormous. I think that the type of person who'd state that life can't be understood, will also say that knowing the purpose of life, is impossible.

I believe that the purpose of life, differs per individual. Not only in this system, which forces us to choose a specialization.

Taking the destructiveness of our current system into consideration, working can't be the purpose of life.

I believe that we're born into a dystopia, which doesn't have an infinite life span. The righteous thing to do, is leave a utopia behind, for our future selves and future generations.

What is the specialization you've chosen, on your current path? What incentivized you to make this decision? The grounds for that choice, must relate to your true purpose.

In our current system, I don't have a specialization. But if I'd be able to conform myself to the routine of the education system for much longer, and not become too distracted with my own ideas, I would get a PhD and specialize in behavioral economics first. In the end, I want to be an authority in every field that exists, because of the system related aspirations I have.

That I think beyond the current system too much to conform myself to it, must relate to my purpose. It's either that, or my life was meant to be short, because I would literally, without a single doubt, rather die than live the same working routine for years, without the system ever changing.

I'm so fed up with the slow process of change, in this system. The future worries me a lot. Trends are about anything, except the mysterious threat of our time. I want to be in charge of our change, and make that a new trend.

I'm a firm believer of sustainably automating jobs, as much as possible, and giving people wealth, based on their contribution to society. For your essentials, you won't have to do anything, because this is an anti-suffering policy! There will be much more time to truly enjoy life. The threat of nature will vanish, too, if this policy is followed well.

To prevent overproduction, we could work with production that is solely based on requests in advance. (And a little bit of emergency supply, depending on what is produced.)

This is all very utopian material, for a chapter of which the title sounds like I was going to discuss "the perfect job" with you. If that's what you're looking for, then we're doing this in an out-of-the-box manner...

Let's disregard the indirect obligation we have, to get access to money. If you get a better income by re-establishing the system from scratch, what would you then want to be in charge of? Or what would you like to have influence in?

Consider the change the system needs, because of the threat of nature – and many more reasons – a puzzle. With my strategy, I could be the frame of the puzzle.

Consider yourself a beautiful puzzle piece. You decide your shape and how you are decorated. Our challenge is to make sure that all pieces and their decorations fit together, and fit the frame.

I won't be telling you how to do your work. All I do is assign a creative (global) challenge to you, from my long list of defined challenges, and make sure that I stay up-to-date with how your process is going. (And assign the right expert to you, to help you, in case you need some assistance.)

It would take too much time, if I'd learn all of the ins and outs of every field this planet knows, to define every piece of the puzzle by myself. That's also a very lonely process... I might not have a cool PhD, but my insight is one-of-a-kind. I hope you will accept me as your Praesens. We'll have a lot of fun together :D.

If you want to change your career around, and you're creative with knowledge, you might want to consider becoming a publicist for D.O.C.I.S. International. Its publications are made to independently influence the process of global change.

With this publication, for example, I'm indirectly attempting to take the lead, in that international process.

D.O.C.I.S. International – the publishing company behind this publication – is my start-up... I'm in desperate need of team members, but I'm very selective, because I really want to succeed...

I'm looking for someone who's very talented... Someone like you! The beginning of our success, is the most fun! The brainstorming, the restless nights, the exploration of our market... You'll love it!

If being a publicist is not for you, then maybe one of the occupations that will come free during our process of actively making changes, might be something for you.

I don't think everyone will appreciate this chapter. (Or any of the chapters in this book.) Someone's occupation, influences his or her status, so this might be a sensitive topic that requires serious attention.

Not everyone will be open to the way I want to change society. Some might even want life to stay exactly the way it is, regardless of the consequences thereof. That's why my system will be parallel, and not a replacement of the current system. It's separation, for those who want that, like me, the way I described it in the chapter about social comfort.

That's also why I need to say the following: no refunds! If this book is purchased for criticism, and not to subject yourself to the challenge within its pages, until you succeed, then the problem is your effort, and not my writing.

When our new system is done, I would love to stay its correspondent, and combine that with my creativity, by making that entertainment. I love making art and making music, aside from writing, finding new knowledge and (the attempt of) making power moves.

Do you agree with what I consider the purpose of life?

If yes: How do you feel about your current specialization? What is your influence, which is portrayed on your puzzle piece, in the puzzle frame metaphor I mentioned in this chapter?

If no: What do you consider the purpose of life?

What are your talents?

Are you currently living life according to your purpose?

What do you want to do after fulfilling your purpose?

What's the difference between now and when you have fulfilled your purpose?

What do you need to do, to fulfill your purpose?

That's how you answer this chapter its lead question.

THE PATH

To generate our (new) path, all we need to do, is place the findings we have examined throughout the previous chapters, in the right order (of paragraphs).

Let's start with labelling them. Please use the following format, where the number (and letter) indicate(s) the label:

1) The description of your current state, including your emotions, your social life and your occupation(s)

2A) Your ideal feelings

2B) The factors that keep away your bad feelings, and what needs to change to make you feel, solely what you want to feel

3A) The description of your ideal social life

3B) The difference between your current and ideal social life, and what would take that difference away

4A) Your ideal that relates to how much power you have in life

4B) Your ideal amount of influence, including if it differs with how it is right now

4C/5C) Your influence in the process of change, from the chapter about power, combined with what you want to be in charge of, as my puzzle piece, if you want to be my puzzle piece, from the chapter about the right occupation

5A) The purpose of life, or your life's purpose

5B) Are you living life according to your purpose? Yes or no

5D) What you need to do to fulfill your purpose

5E) What the difference is between now and when you have fulfilled your purpose

5F) What you want to do after having fulfilled your purpose

5G) What your talents are

The path for a Volta, which will include external factors, is composed according to this format:

*From where I am right now (**1 *description***), to where I want to be, feeling (**2A *list states***), in (**3A *describe social life***), being in control of my life (**4A * "in this way" description***), I know that my purpose in life, is to (**5A *description***).*

To fulfill my purpose in life, and experience eternal happiness, I have designed a path.

The state of my emotions, will be(come) and stay my ideal, when I act upon this: **(2B *description*)**.

I am currently / I am currently not living life according to my purpose **(5B *stripe through what is not applicable*)**. *That's because my purpose is fulfilled when* **(5D *description*)**. *So I need to bridge the gap between / So I have fulfilled my purpose, because* **(5E *stripe through what is not applicable + description*)**.

(This is optional.) *I will intertwine my path with that of Fangs, by* **(4C/5C *description*)**, *because my ideal level of influence is* **(4B *description*)**, *and it will be a fun way to challenge* **(5G *description*)**.

As I walk this path, my social life will become / will stay ideal, by **(3B *description*)**.

When I have fulfilled my purpose, I would love to (5F *description*).

In case you want an example and/or in case you want to know what my Volta is:

My Volta

From where I am right now, to where I want to be, I know that my purpose in life, is to lead the process of global change, on a higher pace.

Currently, I am in Amsterdam, staying with friends of the family, hiding my real feelings, attempting to conform to the social norm, while underneath my façade, I am held captive by feelings of distrust, anger, fear, stress, loneliness, grief and sadness, because at home, the disagreement about what my occupation in life should be, and misuse of authority, make me prefer to be somewhere else, where I can focus on (getting to) my path.

I spend most of my time writing (unpaid). Even though I feel lonely, I prefer to be alone, over being misunderstood and discouraged.

Before the bad publicity, I valued every second I spent with friends and family. Now I avoid them as much as possible. I have seen a side of them, I wish I would have never seen.

Completely distancing myself from them, is not possible yet. Not only because I find it hard to speak these definitive words, because this harshness actually isn't part of my nature. (It's part of my PTSS.)

It's also because our lives are so joined together – even though we have nothing in common – and my façade is so thick, it's not easy to leave this life behind for good. But I want to permanently transfer myself to an environment where I can focus on fulfilling my purpose.

When you don't know about my situation – since I always have been the type of person who keeps to herself – then don't fill things in. Especially not when that can permanently damage my image. I would not do that to anyone. I never expected this from them. They know how high I aim and how much I care about my career. I do not understand how they can believe and tell (me) that I am psychotic, and treat me as such, while they are aware of my intelligence, and the many secrets I still keep to myself.

After two years of celebrating my birthday by myself, I am certain that their love is not real love, for me. (Celebrating my birthday while being unfairly held captive in a mental institution, with a few visitors, is the same as being alone. I used to throw two big parties every year: one for friends and one for family (and family friends).)

This has all become such an enormous burden to me, I can't think or indirectly speak of anything else, most of the time. And I can't talk about it with anyone. I know, because I've tried it, and ended up hurt, every single time.

My love life is on hold, because I still haven't found anyone with a personality that is truly similar to mine – aside from Dr. Crutzen and his fellow Graeynissis [the link refers you to Fangs's Dictionary, on LilFangs.com/fangss-dictionary], who all have very serious occupations. Being around Graeynissis also always makes

me stutter and blush and stuff,
because of my hidden attraction and
distracting thoughts, in that moment.

My current life, without Graeynissis,
sometimes makes me prefer committing
suicide over living, because of the pains
and loneliness, but I don't want to give
up on my purpose, and I don't want
those people I used to trust, to speak
the same untruths over my lifeless
body, the way they spoke about me,
when I was gone (and returned).

My hunger for success and
independence, keep me publishing,
because this is the only occupation
where I'm completely free in what I do
to earn. I never want to work for a
minimum wage again. I don't want to
live any of life's basic routines,
truthfully.

If my Volta becomes successful,
these are my words of goodbye to the

past – truthfully, either way, I'm so done with this life, but my lifeless body is for my Graeynissis, and I want to make sure that that happens. Without any dramatic exchange of words, those who walk this path with me, will know what to do.

I depend on their anticipation, since I don't have a car... Or a house... Or money...

These words are my definitive goodbye to the people from my past. They have never bought any of my books, but in case they suddenly do... I just can't hear argumentation based on: "Life will forever be a dystopia and you a schizophrenic", anymore. It's pointless arguing with that. It might be an emotionally painful read. I wish things would have gone differently, but I can't change what has happened in the past.

I feel like I should compensate them for this, to say that we're even, since not everyone believes in the ending of relationships, but I'm not sure if this is right. Especially because of the financial struggle I've been living through for so many years now, and I need every penny to combine causing the shift, with finally having money to spend on a house etc.

I don't want to complain about the way my life is, anymore. (I never wanted to do that, but I need to air out the pressure on my heart, somehow.) I don't want to be bothered by the stupidities in our system anymore.

I want to experience inner harmony, which will always keep me in balance, feel the continuous arousal that will make life far more exciting, and glow with radiance, which will energize those who I'm around and me.

My social life will be love, business and friendship, together as one, where I will be the leading correspondent of our empire.

To fulfill my purpose in life, and experience eternal happiness, I have designed a path.

I will be able to shift my emotional state and keep my state of bliss, by distancing myself from those who I've spent so much time with, who now have such a permanent negative impact on the way I feel, and creating a new social circle, which will solely consist of those who can hear me reason, and those who don't consider this gift schizophrenia, and who appreciate my work.

I am currently not living life according to my purpose. That's because my purpose is fulfilled, when the new system I have in mind, is established. So I need to find the right people, to fill up my figurative puzzle frame with, which I currently do under the name of Fangs/D.O.C.I.S. International.

As I walk this path, my social life will become ideal, as I fulfill my purpose.

After I have fulfilled my purpose, I would love to stay the leader and correspondent of the new system, while creating new art and entertainment, as a publicist. And I want to have a garden and spend my hours taking care of that...

My dear, I hope you've enjoyed reading this book. I hope it has added something to your life. Most of all, I hope that our paths will intertwine.

Know that by writing down everything that relates to your Volta, you have written down new history! Please, cherish it! You're a pioneer!

At some point in time, I will be collecting success stories, for Part Two of *Volta.* I hope you want to be my co-author! (I'm so sick of writing by myself!!)

The next part of this book, including the details of how the path I've just designed, has played out in real life, will be released within a year from (Wednesday,) January 30, 2019. It depends on how fast my process of finding my companions goes, and the path for global change we design.

Hopefully, by then, I will spend less time writing, and more time being the loving leader of many.

In case you want to keep up with me, before the next part of this book is released: LilFangs.com is updated almost daily. I hope I'll have more interesting content, by the time you visit it.

Currently, in my life as a publisher, I do every single thing by myself. From cover design, to requesting ISBNs, to submitting my works to online stores. And I don't earn from it.

The enormous emotional liability in my life, makes me not share it with people, when I've published something.

Usually, a beginning author gets his or her audience from recommending his or her book to anyone in his or her social circle, and the people from that social circle then recommend the book to their social circle, and so on.

It feels wrong to recommend my book to my social circle, because my burden surfaces in every work, and I end up hurt every time we talk about it – even though I often don't mention that – but I still don't like hurting other people. A definitive goodbye sounds hurtful. But simultaneously, they might not give a fuck, since I've been left alone for so long already. (But every time I see them, they say that they care about me and stuff, which has such a painful impact on my heart. What a topic of conversation... It should be an obvious statement, if we're truly friends, but it feels more like an argument, to convince me, which makes me doubt it even more. I want to talk about what we'll do to the system.)

I can't wait until the expression of my troubled thoughts about my current life, becomes the expression of my learning process, in my new leadership, and all of the fun side-activities we'll do!

The first step of getting towards my Volta, I've taken last week. As I write this, it's Monday, January 28, 05:30 AM, and on Sunday last week, I submitted an alternatively written motivation letter to the Erasmus University, where I used to study. Where Dr. Crutzen works.

For my strategy, I need the right people, money and the acknowledgement of my intelligence. The long way towards this, is by obtaining at least one PhD.

The shorter and more fun way, which suits me better, is by them allowing me to do a research project, under their surveillance. I don't need classes to learn. They work counterproductive, for me.

I learn much and much better, when I need to put the knowledge into practice, in a creative manner.

I want to set up a simulation of the new system I want to create. For both the process of creating it, and for running it. A simple proposal can be found on the D.O.C.I.S. International website.

The (private side of the) university, would be the perfect environment for this. Even though I want to fully distance myself from my past, my B still works there...

I can still hear him through my reasoning. The problem with us might be that when I see him, I'll never want to let him go again, and he might be feeling the same way – I've never had the chance to prove my non-schizophrenia case, so I can't say this with certainty (yet). The problem is that my parents don't approve of him for some reason, and they might accuse him of things that are not true again, and involve the police in this again.

This is such a burden. I miss talking to him. I miss listening to him, even more. (He has such a beautiful accent!)

The publication of *Volta* might be perfect timing. I consciously wrote this exactly now. The concept of the book, has been on my mind for quite some time.

It is meant to show the liabilities of my current life, before the moment has occurred, when my life flips over, to something fun, where I'm living life according to my purpose. And then the next part should show the version of me who is happy and very successful, who will explain the full details about achieving that state.

If the University accepts my offer, and I start with my first official research project, that will be when my Volta kicks in, so the first part of the book, should be published before that.

That's why I wrote this book in a week's time. The admission was spontaneous, and so was this writing.

My books from the Nosce Te Ipsum series aren't selling, so my actual intention was to not publish anything, and rest.

But if my research related offer at the University will be accepted – which is not expected, in my social circle – this *Volta*, will be legendary.

I hope you, my dear reader, will be part of this revolution. May we all see better days!

Thank you so much for reading the first part of *Volta*! With your purchase, you have saved a life.

I love you

- **xxx** -

www.ingramcontent.com/pod-product-compliance
Lightning Source LLC
Chambersburg PA
CBHW021131020426
42331CB00005B/720